THE LITTLE TIN SOLDIER

Om KIDZ
An imprint of Om Books International

Om Kidz | Om Books International

Reprinted in 2020

Corporate & Editorial Office
A-12, Sector 64, Noida 201 301
Uttar Pradesh, India
Phone: +91 120 477 4100
Email: editorial@ombooks.com
Website: www.ombooksinternational.com

Sales Office
107, Ansari Road, Darya Ganj
New Delhi 110 002, India
Phone: +91 11 4000 9000
Email: sales@ombooks.com
Website: www.ombooks.com

Content by Sonia Emm

ISBN: 978-93-84625-15-3

Printed in India

10 9 8 7 6 5 4

THE LITTLE TIN SOLDIER

I'm all set to read

Paste your photograph here

My name is

Chapter 1

THE TIN SOLDIER

"Wow! Tin soldiers!" exclaimed Jack as he opened his birthday gift.

Those were the first words that the twenty-five tin soldiers heard. They were brothers, because they were born from the same tin. They looked alike in their red and blue uniforms with a gun on their shoulder. They stood still and looked ahead.

Except for one tin soldier – he had only one leg as they fell short of tin. But he stood as steady as the others did on two legs. He was the one who went on to become famous too!

Jack arranged the soldiers neatly on a table with all the other toys. There was a big cardboard castle with lots of windows and little trees around it. There was a mirror that resembled a lake. Wax swans swam in the lake and one could see their reflections in the mirror.

But the toy that looked the prettiest was a ballet dancer who stood by the castle doorway. She looked pretty in her white ballerina dress. A blue ribbon curled down her shoulders. Her hair was tied in a neat ponytail and one of her legs was lifted high behind her.

"She too has one leg, just like me! She would be perfect as my wife!" The tin soldier thought. He couldn't see the raised leg from where he stood.

But then he thought, "She's a royal danseuse. I am just a lowly soldier who lives in a cardboard box with twenty four other soldiers. I'm not worthy of her."

He hid behind a box, admiring the dainty lady's beauty. The rest of the tin soldiers went back into their box.

But when night fell and Jack and the rest of his family went to bed, strange things happened in that room.

The toys came to life and started to move and play! The tin soldiers, too, rattled around in their box. They wanted to come out and play with the other toys. The chalks ran around, making patterns on the black slate. The nutcracker hopped around.

They made such a ruckus that the canary bird woke up and started singing! But the ballerina stood on tiptoes with her arms outstretched and the little tin soldier stood staring at her.

Chapter 2

THE SOLDIER FALLS

At midnight, there was a big POP sound. The spice box lid had just flown off. But no spices flew out of it. Out popped a goblin instead!

"Why do you stare at the danseuse like that, tin boy? Turn away or you shall be blown away!" said the sly goblin as he gritted his teeth and slid back into the box.

But the tin soldier ignored him. His gaze was fixed on the lovely lady.

And the night went by.

In the morning, Jack came back and put the tin soldier very close to the window ledge. Sadly, it was a bad day for the little tin soldier. A strong wind blew him off the ledge and out of the window. He fell down and got his head stuck in the bushes, his leg straight up in the air. Jack ran down the stairs with his housemaid to look for him. They looked everywhere but could not find him. Jack went past him but did not notice him.

"If I shout for help, maybe they will find me," thought the tin soldier. But he felt that it was not right to do so, especially while he was still in his uniform.

Soon, it began to rain heavily. Water gushed down the street. Two children noticed the soldier and picked him up.

"Let's sail him in our boat," said one of them. And they did.

They placed the soldier in their paper boat and slid it down a gutter.

The water gushed heavily with the downpour. The boat swirled and was on the verge of being capsized. But the soldier was steadfast. He didn't flinch. He held his head high and went with the flow.

The boys ran along the gutter, clapping as the boat swung from one side to the other. Just then, it hit a plank. All of a sudden, the soldier was in the midst of darkness. This new place was full of rats and other rodents. They tried to gnaw at the boat and tear it. It was their home and they did not like others entering without permission.

But the current was so strong, the boat did not stop. The gutter opened up into a big canal.

THE STRAITS TIMES
ands wet to

Chapter 3

THE SOLDIER'S HEROISM

The water was filling up rapidly in the boat. It was making the paper turn limp. The boat was sinking. The soldier was neck-deep in water. He tried to keep his head up, but the boat sank and the soldier sank deeper and deeper into the water.

He thought of the beautiful ballerina and wished he were with her. He was lost in her thoughts when a giant fish swallowed him up. It was pitch dark inside the fish and still too. But the soldier was brave. He lay there straight, his gun still on his shoulder and his head held high.

The fish squirmed and struggled very awkwardly. Suddenly, it turned still! The tin soldier could feel the fish being dragged out of the water.

He heard a faint voice from far away that was growing louder by the minute.

It said, “Look, what a big fish!”

The fish had been caught by some locals. It was on its way to the market.

“What a fresh catch!” said the housemaid who bought the fish. It was taken straight to the kitchen to be cooked.

The cook cut open the fish and yelled, “A tin soldier! I found a tin soldier!” She removed the tin soldier gently with her fingers. She took him to the people of the house.

And what a coincidence it was! The steadfast tin soldier was in the same toy room where he was first discovered by Jack in his gift box. He saw all his friends and Jack. He looked around for the beautiful castle.

There it was, in the same place, with the charming ballerina still standing by the doorway.

The tin soldier could not have been any happier than he was now.

"I am living a dream," he thought. He had been through many ups and downs after he was removed from the box. But he remained true to his soldier's oath – never give in to any obstacles, overcome them with courage and integrity.

The tin soldier had become soiled and stained after all he had been through. Jack cleaned him up and put him back on the window ledge.

Chapter 4

THE STEADFAST COUPLE

"Don't put him there again, Jack," said Jack's housemaid, who was in the room to clean.

"What if he falls for any reason?"

"You are right, I won't put him by the window again!" replied Jack.

Jack picked up the tin soldier and put him near the castle, right next to the ballerina.

The tin soldier could not believe his luck. He felt that he was being rewarded for braving all the problems he had faced.

The moonlight shone into the room through the window that night. Everyone in the house was fast sleep. But the toys were wide awake. They started playing all over the room. The tin soldier tried to dodge the speeding cars and walking robots.

But he saw something wonderful – he saw the ballerina dance. She was so dainty and graceful, he could not take his eyes off her.

That's when he realised he was wrong about her all this while! The ballerina did not have just one leg like the tin soldier. She had a perfect pair! She had simply lifted one leg behind her to look tiptoed!

"Would you like to dance with me?" the ballerina asked the tin soldier, who was now feeling very shy.

"How can I dance on just one leg?" replied the soldier sadly.

"Only if you try, brave soldier!" said the ballerina, smiling encouragingly at him.

The two danced through the night. The goblin kept out of his way, and yes, they lived happily ever after.